The only thing kids love more than animals is ... BABY animals!

A baby goat is a kid

A baby cow is a calf

A baby pig is a piglet

A baby donkey is a foal

A baby horse is a foal

A baby duck is a duckling

A baby llama is a crias

A baby dog is a puppy

A baby goose is a gosling

A baby rooster is a cockerel

A baby turkey is a poult

A baby rabbit is a kitten

A baby sheep is a lamb

A baby cat is a kitten

Created By

Tomasz Dabrowski

Printed in Great Britain
by Amazon

26108780R00018